Trouble at the Zoo

Written by
Rob Waring and **Maurice Jamall**

Before You Read

to close
something

to pick up
something

to take a
picture

bear

cage

fence

gate

lion

stick

zoo

close/
near

dangerous

loud noise

surprised

scared

worried

"Welcome to Bayview Zoo," says Mr. Jenkins. He works at the zoo.

Today, some students from Bayview High School are at Bayview Zoo.

"Have a good time at the zoo," says Mr. Jenkins.

"But please look at this," he says. He shows them a notice.

The boys and girls look around the zoo. One of the boys is Mike. He sees a lion.

"Look at that lion!" Mike says to his friend, Scott. Mike goes near the lion's cage.

The lion makes a very loud noise at Mike.

Mike says to the lion, "Hey lion, I'm not scared of you!"

A girl watches Mike. She is very worried. Her name is Jenny.

Mr. Jenkins says, "Please do not go near these bears.
They are dangerous."
Mike does not listen to Mr. Jenkins. He picks up a stick.
Mike says to his friend, Scott, "Hey, Scott, watch this!"
He hits the cage with the stick. Now the bear is angry, too.

Mr. Jenkins sees Mike and says, "Stop! Don't do that! Bears are dangerous."

"Sorry, Mr. Jenkins," says Mike. But he is smiling. He is not sorry. Mike gives a sandwich to the big old bear. "Here you are, bears," he says.

Mr. Jenkins sees Mike and says, "Stop that! Sandwiches are very bad for bears. Don't give food to the animals!"

"Sorry," says Mike. But he is not sorry.

"Oh, it's really small," says Jenny's friend, Sarah. She is looking at a baby kangaroo.

The baby kangaroo's name is Joey.

"I want to take a picture with him," she says.

Mr. Jenkins says, "Yes, they're small, but they're very strong. Don't go near them, please."

"Kangaroos are not dangerous," Mike says to Scott. "Look, it's very small."

Mr. Jenkins goes away. Mike goes over the fence. He picks up the baby kangaroo.

"Jenny, do you want a picture with Joey?" asks Mike.

"Stop, Mike, put him down. He doesn't like it," says Jenny.

Jenny goes over the fence to Mike and says,

"Stop it!"

"Put him down, Mike," says Jenny. "Put him down."
Mike says, "It's okay, Jenny. He's okay with me."
But Jenny is angry with Mike. "Give him to me. Now!" she says.
There is a big kangaroo. It is the baby kangaroo's mother.
She looks at Mike.

The kangaroo's mother comes to Mike and Jenny. She does not look happy.

"Look," says Mike. "It's a big kangaroo. Do you want a picture, Jenny?"

Mr. Jenkins sees Jenny and Mike near the kangaroos.

"Jenny! Mike!" he says. "The mother's angry. You have her baby."

The kangaroo comes very close to Mike and Jenny. She is very big. Very, very big.

Mike and Jenny are very worried and scared now.

"I'm scared, Mike. Help me," says Jenny.

Mike is scared too. "Umm . . . Hello, Mrs. Kangaroo," says Mike. "How are you today?" Mike says.

"Umm . . . here, Jenny, you take Joey." He gives the baby kangaroo to Jenny.

The mother kangaroo is very close. She looks down at Mike and Jenny. She is very, very angry.

Mike looks at the mother kangaroo. The mother looks at her baby.

The big kangaroo makes a very loud noise at Mike.

"Let's go! Now! Run, Jenny!" he says.

Mr. Jenkins says, "Stop! No, don't run! Wait there."

Jenny does not run, but Mike runs to the gate. He goes through the gate and closes it.
Jenny is with the very angry kangaroo! She has its baby. And the mother kangaroo wants her baby back!
"Help me, Mr. Jenkins!" she says.

Mr. Jenkins talks to Jenny.

"It's okay, Jenny," says Mr. Jenkins. "You can get out. I can help you."

Jenny says, "I'm scared, Mr. Jenkins. What do I do?"

"Listen to me. Don't run away. Put the baby kangaroo down, Jenny," he says.

Jenny puts the baby kangaroo down. The mother looks at her baby. Then she looks at Jenny.

"Jenny, don't look at the kangaroo," says Mr. Jenkins.
"Now, walk back to me, Jenny." Jenny walks to Mr. Jenkins.
"That's good, Jenny," says Mr. Jenkins. "Don't look at the
mother. Look down, Jenny."
Jenny walks to the gate.
"Good, Jenny," says Mr. Jenkins. "You're very near the gate
now."
He says, "Good. Come out, now, please."

Jenny goes out of the gate. Sarah runs to Jenny. "Are you okay, Jenny?" she asks.

"I'm okay," says Jenny. "Thanks, Mr. Jenkins."

"Good job, Jenny," says Mr. Jenkins.

Mr. Jenkins is very angry with Mike.

"I'm sorry, Mr. Jenkins," says Mike. "I'm sorry, Jenny. I'm really sorry."